CHILDREN IN HISTORY
Tudors

Fiona Macdonald

FRANKLIN WATTS
LONDON·SYDNEY

This edition 2012

First published in 2009 by
Franklin Watts
338 Euston Road
London NW1 3BH

Franklin Watts Australia
Level 17/207 Kent Street
Sydney NSW 2000

ISBN 978 1 4451 0619 9
Dewey classification: 941.05

Series editor: Jeremy Smith
Art director: Jonathan Hair
Design: Jane Hawkins
Cover design: Jane Hawkins
Picture research: Diana Morris

...yright.
please

...ailable

...hildren's

Printed in China

Contents

The Tudors

The Tudor family ruled England from 1485 to 1603. They also ruled Wales from 1536. Tudor kings and queens include some of the most famous names in British history, such as Henry VIII (reigned 1509–1547) and Elizabeth I (reigned 1558–1603).

An ambitious family

The Tudors were a tough, ambitious family, who came to power at the end of a long civil war. They had two main aims. First, to increase the power and importance of the monarchy, and create a strong, central government. Second, they wanted to defend their kingdom from France and Spain, and increase it by conquering its troublesome neighbours, Scotland and Ireland.

▲ A Tudor prince, aged about three, and already dressed in royal robes.

▼ Sir Francis Drake was a brave, skilful sailor, and a pirate.

An age of exploration

Later Tudor rulers, especially Elizabeth I, were keen to support overseas exploration, in the hope of finding silver, gold – and slaves. Tudor seafarers, including Sir Francis Drake (c.1540–c.1596), went on many dangerous voyages. He was the first man to sail around the world.

Artistic times

The Tudor age was also a time of great enjoyment of the arts, and interest in new ideas spread by the latest invention – printing. Kings, queens and rich noble families paid poets, painters and musicians to create works of art. They watched plays and masques (musical entertainments) by dramatists, including William Shakespeare (1564–1616). They wore magnificent fashions, and asked architects and designers to create huge houses and gardens. Many of these stately homes still survive, and we can visit them today.

Religious conflict

Tudor kings and queens found themselves involved in bitter religious quarrels between Roman Catholics, who followed the traditional religion of Britain, and Protestants, who were inspired by new religious ideas. Religion also played an important part in politics. After Henry VIII quarrelled with the Roman Catholic Church in 1534, England was in danger of attack from Catholic countries. Religious differences led to riots, rebellions and plots against the monarchy, and hundreds of people were executed, on royal orders, for their religious beliefs.

▶ In this portrait, Henry VIII stands tall and proud, ready to defend his kingdom.

5

A new baby

The number of babies born to a Tudor woman depended on her rank and wealth. Having babies outside marriage was a religious sin. Unwed mothers were shamed and punished, and struggled to survive.

Rich and poor

Poor women had few babies, with a long gap between each birth. They had to save money until they could afford to get married, usually between the ages of 25 and 30. They breast-fed their babies for at least two years, which they believed prevented pregnancy. By contrast, wealthy noblewomen married young — often in their early teens. They paid wet-nurses to breast-feed their babies. This meant that some noblewomen had a baby almost every year — and died, weak and exhausted, before they were 40.

▶ This baby from a wealthy family is holding a piece of smooth, cool coral. Chewing it helped with teething pain.

Women only

In Tudor homes, childbirth was a time for women only. In rich houses, women stayed in their private rooms for about a month before the baby was due. Poor women worked on farms, as servants, or around the house until it was almost time for their baby to be born. Then they called in women friends to help them, or the local village 'wise woman'.

◀ Nursemaids bathe a newborn baby in a royal lady's bedroom.

A dangerous time

Giving birth was the main cause of death for young women. If they survived, mothers went to church for a special service, to 'purify' them. All babies were baptised (made members of the Christian Church) and were given names by godparents. Saints' names or names from the Bible were the most popular, followed by family names. Godparents were expected to help and protect their godchildren. In wealthy families, they were often powerful friends of the family.

▶ Servants bring food (left) and mix medicine (right) for a woman who has just given birth.

TUDOR LEGACY

Old ideas

Some superstitions surrounding pregnancy and childbirth have survived from Tudor times, or even earlier, and are still remembered today. For example, if a pregnant woman ate too many strawberries, Tudor people said that her baby would be born with a strawberry-shaped birthmark. Women attending a birth might also untie all the knots on clothes and furnishings in a house, and open all the doors and windows, to help the baby be born quickly and without pain.

Family values

Families were vitally important in Tudor times. Without a family, it was impossible for anyone – rich or poor – to survive. Family members provided work, shelter, money, status, comfort and companionship for each other.

The importance of children

Families also needed children, to grow up and support old, frail members of the family, and have more children of their own to continue the family name. Rich, noble families needed male children, as heirs to inherit great estates or kingdoms, and keep the ruling family in power.

▲ A portrait of Anne Boleyn, Henry VIII's second wife, executed at the age of 29.

Needing an heir

King Henry VIII became famous for his desperate wish to have a son and heir to rule after him. Henry's desire to divorce his first wife, who had no surviving sons, led to his quarrel with the Catholic Church in Rome. The beheading of his second wife, Anne Boleyn, who produced only a daughter, and of his fourth wife, who had no children, led to international scandals.

▲ Although this father looks stern, he is holding his sons close, as if to protect them.

Strict parents

Although Tudor families needed children, they did not think it was a good idea to be too kind to them. Fathers and schoolmasters quoted a stern sentence from the Bible: 'Spare the rod and spoil the child.' (It meant: 'If you don't beat children, they'll never learn.') Children, rich and poor, were expected to be obedient to their parents, and to be respectful, religious, honest and hard-working, and to put family interests first, rather than their own wishes.

▶ Fathers led family prayers for the whole family — and the servants.

SIFTING THE EVIDENCE

A Tudor teacher

In 1570, Roger Ascham, who taught Princess Elizabeth before she became queen, wrote a book about bringing up children and teaching them at school. His ideas surprised some of his fellow teachers, but seem sensible to many people today. For example, he wrote, 'the schoolhouse should be a house of play and pleasure, and not of fear... young children were sooner allured (attracted to study) by love, than driven by beating... let him (the teacher) teach the child, cheerfully and plainly (clearly and simply).'

Tudor people

Tudor children had the same wealth and place in society as their parents, and often the same job. It was difficult for a poor person to improve his or her life. A few Tudor people made vast fortunes through trading voyages or war.

Nobles

Around five per cent of the population belonged to noble families. They were enormously wealthy and powerful. Their children lived in huge houses, and would grow up to be Members of Parliament, army commanders, and friends – or enemies – of the royal family.

▶ Hardwick Hall, Derbyshire, was built in the 1590s for the Countess of Shrewsbury.

Middling people

Another 10 per cent of the population were 'middling' (moderately) wealthy. Some were merchants and top craftsmen, others were gentlemen farmers, and some were educated people with responsible jobs, such as lawyers, doctors and churchmen. They hoped their children would follow them into similar jobs.

◀ A portrait of Richard Rich (1496–1567), a well-known Tudor lawyer.

The poor

Compared with noble and 'middling' families, all other Tudor people were poor. They worked as labourers, on farms or in towns, or as servants in richer families' households from a young age. They earned low wages, owned few possessions and lived in small, cramped cottages or rooms in shared houses. Usually, they just about managed to survive and care for their children. But by mid-Tudor times, there was an economic crisis, with even lower wages, high prices and unemployment. Gangs of people roamed the countryside, looking for work – and stealing food to feed their families.

▲ Poor people eating, drinking and quarrelling in a crowded, shabby, dirty inn.

Tudor Poor Laws

Between 1495 and 1597, Tudor governments passed strict new laws to deal with the 'poverty problem'.

- They divided poor people into two groups – the 'deserving poor' (the old, sick or young children) and 'sturdy beggars', who were strong enough to work.

- Local communities had to pay money and provide housing to help their own deserving poor.

- Beggars had to have government permits. Without one, they were whipped and driven out of villages and towns to starve.

Learning

Tudor people believed that education was important, but few people in Tudor society received a proper education. Most noble and middling men and women could read and write, but almost everyone else could not.

Keeping records

Rich families needed to write letters and keep accounts so that they could organise their large households and manage their estates. Government clerks and lawyers had to make neat, careful records of court cases and government decisions. Farmers, craftworkers, traders and shopkeepers all needed to keep notes of buying and selling.

▲ This child is learning the letters of the alphabet from a horn book.

▲ A Tudor printer's workshop. The printing press is on the right.

Learning at home

Rich boys and girls were educated by private tutors at home. As well as learning to read and write, they studied maths, Latin and European languages. Boys and girls from rich families also learned good manners, elegant graceful dancing, and how to give orders to servants or soldiers. The girls were taught fine needlework, and how to make perfumes and remedies. Their brothers practised hunting and fighting.

Going to school

Boys from middling families went to petty (primary) and grammar (secondary) schools. They learned how to read and write, first in English and then in Latin, plus maths and religion. School days were long, and there were classes six days a week, with Sunday free and a half-day on Thursday. Petty schools and grammar schools were run by town councils, private schoolmasters, the Church (until around 1540) and local charities. They charged fees, but had a few free places for poor children. Girls did not go to school, but might be taught to read by their mothers at home.

▼ The Tudor dramatist, William Shakespeare, went to school in this surviving Tudor building.

TUDOR LEGACY

Education and Bible study

By late Tudor times, new Protestant beliefs had become popular in England and Wales. Many Protestants, including people who were not wealthy, wanted to learn to read so that they could study the Bible. (They believed the Bible was the word of God, and should guide their lives; these views have survived, and many people still share them today.) The first English translation of the Bible was printed between 1523 and 1535. The first complete Bible in Welsh was published in 1588.

Useful skills

Poor parents could not afford to send their children to school. Tudor schools charged fees and books were expensive. Instead, poor children learned useful skills whilst working alongside their parents, or became apprentices.

Skills for the poor

Girls were taught cooking, cleaning, baby-care, how to wash and mend clothes, spin and weave cloth, raise chickens, milk cows, make butter and cheese, and grow vegetables in kitchen gardens. Boys learned building and gardening, how to grow crops, drive horse-drawn ploughs and carts, and how to care for farm animals.

▼ A farmer's son feeds the chickens on a snowy day.

▲ A master clockmaker (right) gives instructions to two workmen and (in the background) an apprentice.

Learning a trade

If boys were not needed to help their parents, they left home at around 10 years old. They found work as servants in richer households, or, if they were lucky, became apprentices. Apprentices lived in the home of a master craftsman or trader, worked with him and learnt his skills. Being an apprentice was a great opportunity. Skilled craftsmen, merchants and shopkeepers were some of the richest people in Tudor towns.

Master-craftsmen

After seven years, an apprentice was free to leave his master and work for anyone who would pay him. If he was very skilled, after seven more years he might produce an extra-special piece of work, his 'masterpiece', and be recognised as a master-craftsman. Most apprentices were boys but a few girls became apprentices to portrait painters, embroidery experts or lace-makers.

▶ This splendid silver chalice, a cup for holding holy wine in church, shows the high standards achieved by Tudor master-craftsmen.

SIFTING THE EVIDENCE

Apprenticeship agreements

When a boy or girl became an apprentice, they signed an agreement, called an 'indenture' with their master. Some indentures have survived.

Usually, they agreed to:
- Serve their master well
- Obey his orders
- Keep their master's trade secrets
- Look after their master's belongings
- Live good, moral lives
- Not get married
- Keep away from pubs
- Not play cards or dice or gamble.

In return, their master promised to:
- Give them food, clothes and shelter
- Teach them the skills of his trade
- Sometimes, pay them low wages (many apprentices were unpaid)
- Not harm them.

Food and drink

For the first two years of life, babies were breast-fed. As they grew older, they were fed purees and gruel. By around four or five years old, children ate the same food as their parents.

Food for the poor

Poor people's food was stodgy and dull. Meals were based on coarse brown bread, or porridge stewed over an open fire. There might also be soup or pudding made from dried peas, onions and herbs. In season, Tudor people enjoyed stewed fruit or boiled vegetables. Bacon, smoked sausage and eggs were treats. Weak beer was drunk by everyone, even children.

▲ Poor people cooked over open fires. Here a cauldron hangs over the flames.

Food for the rich

Rich families ate more, but their diet was not healthy. It was based on meat, with only a little bread, fruit and vegetables. Wine was the fashionable drink. Very rich people could afford sugar — a new luxury from the Middle East and America. Elizabeth I's teeth rotted and went black because she ate so much of it.

◀ Servants hard at work in the kitchen of a rich family's home.

Entertaining

Entertaining was important as a way of making helpful friendships. Nobles employed lots of kitchen helpers to prepare splendid feasts. Young servant girls peeled vegetables and washed dishes, boys turned spits on which meat was roasted and waited at table. Many dishes were elaborately decorated. Tudor diners enjoyed edible jokes, like animals made of pastry then filled with red wine. When 'stabbed' with a knife or an arrow, the wine ran out, like blood!

▼ Tudor villagers celebrated festivals with feasts, music and dancing.

TUDOR LEGACY

Tudor food

Tudor people did not like waste, and ate as much as they could of any animal killed for food. Today, butchers still sell a few items that Tudor children would enjoy: calves' tongues, pigs' trotters (toes), black pudding (made with blood), sausages (made with chopped meat scraps) and – in Scotland – haggis. This is made of a sheep's stomach filled with its chopped lungs, liver and heart, all mixed with oatmeal. Modern shops also sell another Tudor favourite: marchpane (marzipan). This is a sweet, sticky paste made of ground almonds mixed with sugar and flavoured with rose water. Tudor cooks moulded it into amazing shapes, and decorated it with real gold.

Looking good

The Tudor age was a time when people liked to display their wealth and rank by wearing elaborate clothes made of costly fabrics and decorated with luxury items such as gold thread, pearls and fur.

Lots of layers

Until boys and girls were about five years old, they wore the same kind of clothes — layers of long, loose tunics, reaching below the knees, tied round the waist with a fabric belt or cord. To keep out the cold, they wrapped a cloak (if they were rich) or scrap of old blanket (if they were poor) around their shoulders and wore a close-fitting hat or bonnet. Rich children wore shoes and hand-knitted stockings (long socks) — a new, expensive fashion. Poor children wore boots or went barefoot.

Working clothes

Poor and middling people's clothes were looser — they needed room to move, for work — and were made of tougher, plainer fabric. A boy wore a loose shirt, baggy breeches (shorts) and a jacket. A girl wore a loose shirt under a dress, or with a waistcoat and a long skirt that ended above the ankles, so that it would not trail in the mud.

▲ A painting called *Marriage at Bermondsey* showing clothing typical of the period.

▲ Young children would have worn loose-fitting cloaks like the ones shown here.

18

Clothes for the wealthy

When a boy reached five or six, he was given his first pair of trousers. This was called 'breeching'. From the age of six, children's clothes were smaller versions of adult styles. For rich boys, this meant a shirt topped by a tight-fitting jacket worn with breeches (shorts). A rich girl wore a long shift (like a nightdress), an under-dress, an outer dress with a long, stiff skirt and very tight sleeves and bodice, and a face-framing hat with a veil trailing behind. Stylish clothes were padded, decorated, slashed (had little cuts with contrasting fabric showing through) and embroidered. Ruffs — wide, stiff, frilly collars — were the fashion in late Tudor times.

▶ This young boy proudly wears his first pair of breeches.

Queen Elizabeth I, as described by some Tudor writers

'Slender (slim) and straight; her hair inclined to pale yellow; her forehead large and fair; her eyes lively and sweet but short-sighted, her nose somewhat rising in the midst; her countenance (face) was somewhat long, but yet of admirable beauty, in a most delightful composition of majesty and modesty...'
Sir John Hayward, an Elizabethan Historian

'Her bosom was uncovered (she wore a low-cut robe), as all the English ladies do till they marry. Her hands were slender, her fingers rather long... her appearance was dignified, and her manner of speaking mild and obliging.'
Paul Hentzner, a visitor to Elizabeth I's court

Fun and games

Tudor children had some free time to play on Sundays and holy-days (holidays). These were times for fairs, with stalls, sideshows, jugglers, acrobats and tricksters. Tudors also enjoyed pre-Christian festivals, such as May Day and Halloween.

At home

At home, children played with rag dolls, carved wooden animals, spinning tops, hoops, skittles and balls. They might meet their friends to play blind-man's buff or 'tag', or team games such as tug-of-war. They played drums, whistles, viols (rather like violins) and gitterns (early guitars). Tudor children (and adults) also enjoyed some entertainments that we would find very cruel today, such as bear-baiting (fights between bears and big dogs) — and public executions!

▲ A wealthy noble gallops through the countryside on his horse.

Pursuits for the rich

Jesters amused rich children at royal palaces and nobles' houses. Some large houses had tennis courts. Tudor tennis players hit the ball across a net, but also bounced it off the walls and the floor of an indoor court. Rich children rode on horseback, chasing small birds with hawks or hunting deer.

▼ This rich Tudor girl is holding her favourite doll, also dressed in the latest fashion.

Sports and games

In villages, poor men and boys got together to play rough, rowdy games of football. Teams could be any size; players ran through the streets and the goal posts might be a kilometre or more apart. Games could last all day, and players could throw, kick or pick up the ball. Sometimes, games turned into riots. In the early 16th century, Henry VII tried to ban football and many other games, without much success. He ordered men and boys to 'work more and play less', and to practise shooting with bows and arrows, to be ready to go to war.

▶ How many games can you see being played in this painting from the Tudor era.

SIFTING THE EVIDENCE

Boy actors

In cities and towns, older children might also visit exciting new theatres. Laws banned women from acting in public, so teenage boys took women's parts. Here is how the boy playing Desdemona (the murdered heroine in *Othello*, one of Shakespeare's most famous plays) was described in 1610:

'She/he always acted the part very well, and her death on stage was very moving. While stretched out on her deathbed, she made the audience pity her just by the expression on her face alone.'

Family prayers

Religion played a very important part in Tudor people's lives. Everybody believed in God and the Devil. Adults and children felt passionately about rival Protestant and Catholic beliefs, and were prepared to die for them.

Heaven and Hell

Parents, priests and schoolmasters taught boys and girls that God saw everything they did. Bad deeds would be punished in Hell, but good deeds would be rewarded in Heaven. This was terrifying for some Tudor children, but comforted others. Families prayed together before meals, and parents told their children stories from the Bible or about saints' lives, as examples of good behaviour to follow.

▲ Tudor artists showed Hell as an angry monster, waiting to eat people who behaved badly.

Church and law

Church and state worked together to control Tudor people. By law, all Tudor people — even children — had to go to their parish (local) church every Sunday. They could be fined — or imprisoned — for staying away, and executed for spreading religious beliefs that did not fit in with those of the reigning monarch.

◄ Some people were burnt at the stake for not following the correct religious beliefs.

Tudor witches

Tudor people believed in magic and witchcraft. Many witches were harmless, selling healing remedies or lucky charms. But some adults and children said that witches had evil powers, and were afraid of them. Tudor governments also thought that witches were dangerous and passed laws to punish or execute them.

In 1566, for example, 18-year-old Joan Waterhouse, of Chelmsford, Essex, admitted that she had 'called up' the Devil, in the shape of a dog with horns, to curse a neighbour's child who had refused to give her bread when she was hungry. Joan was found not guilty. But Joan's mother, Agnes, was accused of using her devilish cat to curse farmers' cattle. She was hanged.

Cradle to the grave

The Church held services for all the most important occasions in families' lives: baptisms, marriages and funerals. It investigated and punished moral crimes, such as swearing, telling lies and sex outside marriage. But it also gave help to many Tudor people. There were church charities, church hospitals and church almshouses (homes for old, sick people). Fairs took place in churchyards, close to the burial plots of dead villagers.

▼ The parish church was at the centre of Tudor life.

23

Growing up

Families ate meals together, worked together and spent free time together. Brothers or sisters, or young male or female servants, shared rooms and even beds. Young people were kept busy, and they had to be obedient.

Living together

Rich or poor, young people lived in their family or employer's home until they got married. Tudor people thought that it would be wrong to leave home before then — and poor young people could not earn enough to pay rent of their own, anyway.

▲ Closely surrounded by her children, this Tudor noblewoman beams with joy.

▲ Young, betrothed couples stroll through a garden.

Marriage

Most boys and girls were not free to choose their own marriage partners. Rich, noble families arranged marriages between their children for political reasons, or to make money. Heirs and heiresses who would inherit great estates might be betrothed (engaged) soon after they were born. Even poor families took care over the choice of a husband or wife for their children. Marrying a husband with property was one of the few ways in which a poor Tudor girl could hope to grow richer.

Marrying young

The legal age of marriage was 12, but few Tudor children got married quite so young. Very rich boys and girls often wed between the ages of 14 and 16. Children from poorer families waited until they had enough money to marry – usually, in their late twenties – or until their parents died and they could take over the family home. Divorce was almost impossible but many marriages did not last a lifetime because the husband or wife died young.

▶ A 16th-century illustration showing a young woman taking her wedding vows.

TUDOR LEGACY

Getting married

All Tudor couples had to marry in church. Here is part of the Marriage Service printed in 1559, in the original Tudor spelling. Church wedding services, and some civil wedding ceremonies, use similar words today:

'Wylt thou have thys woman to thy wedded wyfe, to lyve together after Goddes ordynaunce in the holye estate of Matrimony? Wylt thou love her, comforte her, honour, and kepe her, in sickenes, and in healthe? And forsakyng al other, kepe the onely to her, so long as you both shall live?'

To understand the spelling, try reading the text out loud. Wylt = will; thou = you; Goddes = God's; ordynance = law; estate = status; kepe the onely = be faithful.

Not forgotten

Childhood was a dangerous time for Tudor boys and girls. Four out of ten babies did not survive to reach five years old. Another one in ten probably died before they reached 16.

A dangerous time

Some babies perished in the first few weeks of life, from conditions that can be cured by drugs or operations today. Others were killed by coughs, colds and common illnesses. When babies grew old enough to crawl, new dangers threatened them. All Tudor homes had open fires; some also had steep stairs, open windows, wells or ponds, and were surrounded by deep moats or ditches. Once children began to eat solid food, they were at risk from food-poisoning and from sickness and diarrhoea caused by dirty, polluted water.

▲ This stone-carving shows good dead children, left, going to Heaven, and bad dead children, right, going to Hell.

Deadly diseases

Like all other Tudor people, children were at great risk from infectious diseases. Smallpox and deadly bubonic plague were the most dangerous, but measles and 'flu also killed thousands.

▼ A child's gravestone at the Sibbaldbie and Johnstone Church of Scotland.

Remembering the dead

Even though deaths were so common, Tudor parents mourned their children. Their Christian beliefs encouraged them to hope that the children's souls would live on. If they were rich, they paid for tombs, carved with a child's portrait and the dead child's name. These images formed a comforting link between the living and the dead. Some parents also named new babies after dead older brothers or sisters. Perhaps this was just a memorial, or perhaps they hoped that the dead child's soul would somehow come to guide and protect the new baby.

▶ This Tudor tombstone shows a teenager as his parents wanted to remember him.

A Tudor child's death and funeral

A Tudor account, written in 1509, tells of the death of a young servant boy working at a university college in Oxford. He became ill. The college bought medicine for him (treacle, which was meant to be good for the digestion) and hired a nurse to sit with him for two days and two nights. Sadly, the boy died, but the college was determined to give him a respectful funeral – which perhaps shows how much he was missed. The college paid for candles to burn around his dead body, for mournful church bells to be rung, for a solemn funeral service and prayers, for a shroud to wrap his body and for digging his grave.

Activities

Here are some activities for you to try, based on the Tudor period.

Make a Tudor miniature

Tudor men and women loved to wear miniatures, little portraits of close friends, on ribbons round their necks or pinned to their clothes. The finest miniatures had gold or silver frames, decorated with jewels.

You will need:

• A photo or a small portrait (you can draw one).

• A circle of cardboard around 6–8 cm in diameter (make sure it is bigger than the photograph you are using)

• Hole punch. • Ribbon or cord.

• Scissors. • Glue.

• Gold or silver paint and paintbrush.

• Plastic 'jewels'.

1. Trim the photo to fit the circle of card and stick it on top.

2. Punch a hole at the top of the card.

3. Paint a 'frame' all round the edge of the circle.

4. When the paint is dry, stick 'jewels' all round the card.

5. Thread cord or ribbon through the punched hole.

Practise beautiful writing

Tudor kings, queens and scholars used a beautiful new style of handwriting based on ancient Roman carved inscriptions. Today, this style of writing still survives, and is called 'italic'. Elizabeth I was famous for her signature which was decorated with patterns based on italic handwriting.

Look at the italic alphabet and try to write your name in italics and decorate your signature with italic designs.

aabcdefghijklmnopqrstu vwxyz

ABCDEEFGHIJKLMN OPPQRSTUVXYZ

Make a marchpane rose

The Tudor Rose (a flat, open rose with red and white petals) was the symbol of the Tudor monarchs. It was used to decorate Tudor buildings, monuments, clothes — and food.

Marchpane (marzipan) was a favourite Tudor sweet, but only rich people could afford it.

You will need:

- A packet (around 200 g) of prepared marzipan.

- About 25 g icing sugar

- Edible food colouring (red and yellow).

- Clean chopping board (NOT one used for meat or fish).

- Clean plate.   • Rolling pin.

- Clean cotton buds.

- Circular pastry cutter around 2.5 cm in diameter.

Method:

1. Sprinkle half the icing sugar onto the board, and the rest over the rolling pin.

2. Roll the marzipan until it is about 1 cm thick, or less.

3. Use the pastry cutter to cut out 11 circles into the shape of petals.

4. Arrange the circles on the plate to make petals, as shown.

5. Using cotton buds, colour the petals red.

6. Colour the central circle yellow.

Tudor music

If you play a musical instrument, ask your music teacher or a librarian to help you find some Tudor music to play. The most famous Tudor tune is 'Greensleeves'. It may have been written by King Henry VIII.

Timeline

1485 Battle of Bosworth Field. End of the Wars of the Roses. Henry VII becomes the first Tudor king.

1492 Christopher Columbus sails across the Atlantic Ocean, and returns with news of the American continent.

1509 Henry VII dies. His son, Henry VIII, becomes king.

1533 Henry VIII marries his second wife, Anne Boleyn. (He later marries four more times.)

1534 Henry VIII quarrels with the Pope and declares that he is the supreme head of the Church in England.

1535 The first English Bibles are issued to parish (local) churches.

1536 The kingdoms of Wales and England are united.

1536–1539 Henry VIII closes down all monasteries in England.

1541 Henry VIII declares that he is King of Ireland.

1542 Mary Queen of Scots claims the right to rule in England.

1547 Henry VIII dies, and his son, Edward VI becomes king.

1548 Edward VI's government orders everyone in England to worship using a new, Protestant, prayer book.

1553 Edward VI dies.

1553 Henry VIII's elder daughter, Mary I, becomes queen. She is a Catholic, and brings back Catholic ways of worshipping.

1558 Mary I dies, and Henry VIII's youngest daughter, Elizabeth I, becomes queen. She is a Protestant.

1577 Sir Francis Drake completes his round-the-world-voyage.

1587 Elizabeth I executes Mary Queen of Scots.

1588 England defeats the Spanish Armada (a battle fleet).

1591 William Shakespeare's first play is performed in London.

1598 A new Poor Law sets out tough punishments for beggars.

1603 Queen Elizabeth I dies.

Glossary and further information

almshouses homes for old or sick people.

apprentice young person who works with an older, well-trained person, to help them and learn their skills.

baptised made a member of the Christian Church.

Bible the Christian holy book.

breeches knee-length trousers or shorts.

c. short for 'circa', it means around this date.

dramatist someone who writes plays.

horn book words or letters marked on wood and protected by a thin layer of animal horn.

infections disease a disease that spreads easily from person to person.

jester an entertainer who tries to make people laugh.

masques musical entertainments, with singing, dancing and special effects.

middling in the middle – quite wealthy people, later to be called the middle class.

monarchy government by kings or queens.

Protestants Christians who worship in a simple way, and are led by the teachings of the Bible.

puree food that has been made smooth.

rank place in society, similar to class.

remedies medicines.

Roman Catholics Christians who follow the leadership of the Pope in Rome, Italy.

soul departed spirit of a person.

wet-nurse a woman who breast-feeds another mother's baby.

wise woman a traditional healer.

Finding out more about life in Tudor England

Here are some museums and websites that you can visit to find out more about Tudor life:

Hampton Court Palace

Built by Thomas Wolsey, this became one of Henry VIII's favourite royal palaces.

www.tudorbritain.org

A fascinating interactive website produced by the National Archives and the Victoria and Albert Museum.

www.nmm.ac.uk/TudorExploration/NMMFLASH

A fun website about Tudor exploration from the National Maritime Museum, London.

Index